EARLY PARABOLIC SCHEME
PARABOLIC RIDGE PROFILE
PARABOLIC RIB PROFILE
SINGLE SKIN R.C. SHELL WITH RIBS
RED BOOK FEB 1958

1958

ELLIPSOID SCHEME
ELLIPTICAL RIDGE PROFILE

1961

...HEME
...IDGE PROFILE
...RIB PROFILE
...ECAST R.C.
...T 1961

1961

FINAL SPHERICAL SCHEME
SMALL CIRCLE RIDGE PROFILE
GREAT CIRCLE RIB PROFILE
PRECAST R.C. PARTIALLY INSITU
ALL WORKING DRAWINGS 1962-63

**1962
-63**

Sydney Opera House
idea to icon

Michael Moy

SYDNEYOPERAHOUSE

'The idea has been to let the platform cut through like a knife, and separate primary and secondary function completely. On top of the platform the spectators receive the completed work of art and beneath the platform every preparation for it takes place.'

Jørn Utzon, 1965

British sails in Sydney Cove

On a summer day a little over two hundred years ago, *HMS Supply*, under the command of Captain Arthur Phillip, cut through the heads of a magnificent and secure harbour the winds of which had never before touched canvas and dropped anchor in a small, deep cove. The next morning, 26 January 1788, Phillip went ashore, and with the local Cadigal people watching from a distance, planted a flag claiming the land for King George III. *Supply* was soon joined by the other vessels of the First Fleet, and over the next few days, the human cargo, consisting of seven hundred and thirty convicts exiled from England for mostly petty crime, went about unloading provisions, clearing land and erecting shelters under the guard of the British marines. A prefabricated canvas Government House was set up on the site now occupied by the Museum of Sydney while convict accommodation was established to the west in the area which became known as The Rocks. The activities marked a new beginning for the ship-weary arrivals and an end

Bennilong

Bennilong, a native of New Holland, who after experiencing for two years the luxuries of England, returned to his own country and resumed all his savage habits

to a way of life for the Cadigal and their neighbours.

In late 1789, with Sydney Cove settlement firmly established, Governor Phillip undertook a further challenge assigned by King George: 'to open an intercourse with the natives, and to conciliate their affections.' Frustrated by failure to achieve this objective using conventional techniques, Phillip ordered kidnappings and two Wangal men, Bennelong and Colbee, were captured at Manly Bay. Colbee soon escaped but Bennelong remained and proved to be just the person Phillip needed. Housed at Government House, Bennelong learned the English language and ways, even dressing as an Englishman; in turn, Phillip absorbed much about Aboriginal culture from his captive guest. Bennelong was both intelligent and astute, making use of his acquired skills to facilitate trade between his people and the newcomers, thereby benefiting the clan and elevating his standing within it. In the autumn of 1790, Bennelong escaped and returned to his people. When Phillip visited Manly Bay in the hope of re-establishing the relationship, he was speared by one of Bennelong's friends. Further bloodshed was avoided when Phillip accepted Bennelong's pleading that the attack had been the result of a misunderstanding. A truce was subsequently negotiated outlawing such kidnapping and allowing Bennelong and his clan open access to the settlement at Sydney Cove. The following year Phillip had a house built for Bennelong and his family on Cattle Point, the eastern peninsula of Sydney Cove, which became known as Bennelong Point.

When the time came for Phillip to return to England after almost five years in the colony, Bennelong, eager for adventure, accepted an invitation to join him. In England, Bennelong met King George, visited Parliament and learned to box, skate, and drink more than the moderate amounts he had enjoyed at Sydney Cove. In 1795 he returned to his homeland a torn man, fitting in with neither his own people nor the Europeans. He died at Kissing Point in January 1813.

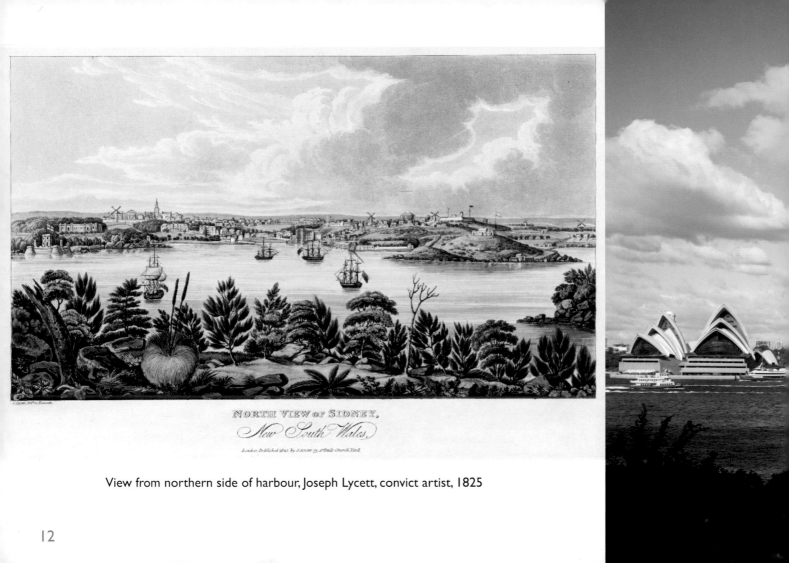

NORTH VIEW OF SIDNEY,
New South Wales

London Published 1825 by J. Souter 73 St Pauls Church Yard

View from northern side of harbour, Joseph Lycett, convict artist, 1825

Guns and trams

The architectural history of Bennelong Point dates from 1817 when the colony's fifth governor, Lachlan Macquarie, assigned convict Francis Greenway the task of building a fort on the small island off the tip of the point. Greenway, a qualified architect, had been transported to Sydney Cove to serve a fourteen year sentence for forging a solicitor's signature. Fort Macquarie, one of a number of projects undertaken by Greenway, was established to guard against clandestine departures by sea and protect the colony from enemies of England. The island upon which the fort was built became part of the peninsula when a drawbridge was replaced by rock fill. Fort Macquarie, from which no shot was ever fired in anger, was demolished in 1901 to make way for a red brick and sandstone tram depot which featured decorative towers and parapets designed to disguise the ugly but functional sawtooth roof a mere 200m from Government House. With the phase-out of Sydney's trams, Fort Macquarie Depot was closed in October 1955 and demolished three years later to make way for an opera house.

The conductor and his dream

In 1946 English composer and conductor Eugene Goossens arrived in Sydney at the invitation of the Australian Broadcasting Commission to conduct a series of concerts around Australia. Time would see him do much more. The very talented Goossens had spent the previous twenty years in the United States, initially at the invitation of Kodak founder George Eastman as conductor of the Eastman-Rochester Philharmonic Orchestra, and later as conductor of the Cincinnati Symphony Orchestra. Both orchestras performed in purpose-built halls with seating capacities in the order of 3500. At the end of his Australian tour, Goossens was offered two prestigious positions: Director of the New South Wales Conservatorium of Music and Chief Conductor of the Sydney Symphony Orchestra. Keen for a new challenge and liking what he had seen of Australia, Goossens accepted both and set to work in July 1947. His ability to attract overseas talent and produce more challenging works saw Sydney Symphony Orchestra subscriptions double in a very short time. As well as attracting internationally acclaimed staff to the conservatorium, Goossens taught some classes himself and staged a number of operas including his own, *Judith*, casting Sydney stenographer Joan Sutherland as lead, a performance that helped spark a stellar career.

Only the lack of a purpose-built performance space stood in the way of Goossens fulfilling an early-stated goal to make the Sydney Symphony Orchestra one of the best in the world. In those days, symphony concerts were held in Sydney Town Hall, a venue with a seating capacity of 2300, no heating, and no facilities for providing refreshments, the latter deficiency causing patrons to dash to pubs and cafes during intermission. Goossens outlined a vision for an acoustically perfect concert hall with seating for 3500, a home for an opera company, and a smaller hall for chamber music. This vision gained enthusiastic support from University of Sydney's Henry Ingham Ashworth and George Molnar who assigned fifth-year architecture students the task of designing an opera house at Bennelong Point. The best of the students' work was displayed at David Jones department store in 1951. The ball had been set rolling.

The visionary politician

John Joseph Cahill was born in inner-city Redfern in 1891 to Irish working-class parents. Upon completion of his schooling at the age of sixteen, Joe, as he was commonly known, joined the state railways as an apprentice fitter. Driven to better himself, he attended lectures organised by the Workers Educational Association and developed skills as a debater. His first political position was as a branch officer with the Amalgamated Society of Engineers. Involvement in a strike in 1917 saw him dismissed from the railways with his personnel file marked 'agitator'; later action against the union's governing body saw him banned from it. A failed attempt to win a seat in state parliament in 1917 was followed by lean years before he was re-employed by the railways. In 1925 Cahill made a second run for state parliament and was elected. When Goossens arrived on the Sydney cultural scene two decades later, Cahill was a government minister with several large infrastructure projects to his credit including the State Dockyard at Newcastle and the electrification of much of rural New South Wales. A keen proponent of the view that grand projects should be matched by progress in cultural opportunities, Minister Cahill was just the ally Eugene Goossens needed. In 1952 Cahill became premier and two years later called a public meeting to consider the building of an opera house in Sydney. At that meeting Goossens outlined ideal sizes for the various types of theatres and a working committee was set up to move the project forward and advise the government. The Opera House Committee had five members: Eugene Goossens and Professor Ashworth were joined by General Manager of the Australian Broadcasting Commission (ABC), Charles Moses; Town Clerk, Roy Hendy; and Under-Secretary for Local Government, Stan Haviland. The Committee considered a number of sites for the proposed opera house including Bennelong Point, The Domain, the Haymarket district near Central railway station, and Phillip Park near St Mary's Cathedral. On 17 May 1955 the government announced that Bennelong Point was the site upon which the opera house would be built.

The competition

With the site of the opera house determined, the Committee set about drafting guidelines for a design competition. Should the competition be restricted to Australian architects? Should it be by invitation or open to anyone? Who should judge the entries? After some deliberation, the Committee decided upon an international open competition with the identities of the entrants not revealed to the judges. George Molnar had argued that this was the best way for 'magnificent, lonely ideas' to get an airing. The competition for the design of the National Opera House with a first prize of $10,000 was advertised internationally in December 1955 with deadlines of 15 March 1956 for registration and 3 December 1956 for submission of designs. The competition book, which became known as the Brown Book, sent to 722 interested parties upon payment of the $20 registration fee, included black and white photographs of the site along with dimensions and specifications. There would be two large halls: a major hall seating between 3000 and 3500 for symphony concerts, large scale operas, ballet and dance performances, choral performances, pageants and mass meetings; and a minor hall with seating for 1200 for dramatic presentations, intimate operas, chamber music performances, recitals and lectures.

In all, 222 schemes were submitted from twenty-eight countries including sixty-one from Australia; fifty-three from the United Kingdom; twenty-four from the United States, twenty-three from Germany and two from Denmark. The judging panel consisted of two local architects and two internationals: Henry Ashworth, the Opera House Committee member chiefly responsible for setting up the competition and selecting the international panel members; Cobden Parkes, the New South Wales Government Architect; Leslie Martin, Chief Architect to the London County Council; and Finnish-American, Eero Saarinen. Martin had been responsible for London's Royal Festival Hall which opened in 1951 and Saarinen, winner of the competition for the St Louis Gateway Arch ten years earlier, had recently designed the TWA Terminal at New York's Idlewild (now JFK) Airport, a structure which incorporated the latest concrete shell technology. Judging took place at the Art Gallery of New South Wales in January 1957.

Images of site from Brown Book

A scandal, a loss

The competition underway, Eugene Goossens left Australia to be knighted by Queen Elizabeth II at Buckingham Palace and to undertake a brief European concert tour unaware that the New South Wales police were investigating his private life. An interest in the occult had led Goossens to an involvement with Rosaleen Norton, a self-professed witch and practitioner of sex magic. Tipped off about this relationship, a reporter took the matter to the police who searched Norton's Kings Cross flat and found explicit letters supposedly written by Goossens. These letters, along with some photographs obtained from another source, were enough for the police to consider charging Goossens with scandalous conduct. *The Sun* newspaper had Goossens followed in London and details of his visits to sex shops in Soho were reported to the Sydney office. When Goossens returned to Australia on 9 March 1956, customs, the police and a *Sun* photographer were waiting. A search of Sir Eugene's bags revealed photographs, books and film of a pornographic nature. Humiliated by the publicity, Sir Eugene resigned from his positions with the orchestra and conservatorium and faced the court to be fined $200 for importing prohibited material. He was never charged with scandalous conduct, a charge which exists today but with a much higher threshold than in 1956. Sir Eugene left Australia in May 1956 and died in England six years later as his dream project was well and truly underway.

The magnificent, lonely idea

Jørn Utzon was born in Copenhagen on 9 April 1918 and spent his formative years in Helsingør where his naval architect father was the director of a shipyard. A keen sailor, Utzon initially considered a career in the navy, but summers spent at the shipyard with his father, drawing plans and making models, convinced him that his future lay in architecture, a decision which saw him gain entry to the Royal Academy of Arts in Copenhagen. Upon graduation in 1942 he left German-occupied Denmark to work in neutral Sweden, and at war's end, Finland, before returning to Denmark to set up his own practice. Utzon was a keen traveller, visiting countries as varied as Morocco, the United States, Mexico, Japan and China during his early years, studying culture and design. Between 1944 and 1956, sometimes in partnership with other architects, he entered twenty or so competitions ranging from London's Crystal Palace competition ten years after the original structure burned down to a competition for the design of a Danish crematorium. Although he won seven of the competitions, none resulted in a commission to carry out the work. A Swedish competition for affordable courtyard housing was particularly close to his heart. His design, influenced by Chinese farm houses which were closed to the outside but opened to a central courtyard, won the competition but was not built. Determined to see his concept realised, Utzon took his prize-winning plans to the Mayor of Helsingør who approved what became the Kingo project, sixty-three affordable dwellings on an undulating four hectare site. This project, which was delivered on budget, led to other work including a housing project in Fredensborg.

His imagination fired by the National Opera House Competition, Utzon spent weeks researching the site, Sydney and Australia. To supplement the competition information in the Brown Book, he visited the Australian Embassy in Copenhagen to view a film about Sydney and look through its collection of books and brochures. He also obtained maritime charts of Sydney Harbour to measure distances and better visualise the relationship between the site and its surroundings. What struck him most was the similarity between Bennelong Point and the peninsula at Helsingør around which he often sailed, a peninsula dominated by magnificent Kronborg Castle, famous as the setting for Shakespeare's *Hamlet*. 'I stood looking at clouds over a low coastline, and I had a look at Kronborg Castle at Helsingør, and at Gothic churches. There you have forms against a horizontal line like the sea or the clouds without a single vertical line, nothing constituting weight, and with forms that are different from all angles.'

Utzon realised that, as with Kronborg Castle, Sydney Opera House would be viewed from all sides, and also from the Sydney Harbour Bridge deck and Royal Botanic Gardens above. How then to disguise the above-stage fly towers and other mundane but essential features? Sydney Opera House could not have an ugly side, not even an ugly roof. Sails on the water and the wings of a swan provided the answer. Shells would cover the halls and fly towers above the stages. And the halls would be placed side by side, not end to end, even though this resulted in a total width greater than that specified in the competition rules. The stages would be placed at the southern end, the direction from which the audience would approach in 'festive procession'. The approach would be easy, as in Grecian theatres, using uncomplicated stairway constructions. Stairs to the theatre lobbies at the northern end overlooking the harbour would, of necessity, run beside the stages. And fire escape doorways would link the theatre interiors to the stairs allowing a speedy evacuation if necessary. What then of the stage wings, the spaces to the side where sets are stored ready to be moved on stage when needed? Scenery would be brought to the stage from below by

Kronborg Castle, Denmark

mechanical lifts. And beneath the shells: '... because the site was rather small, I came to the conclusion that I would have to make one architectural unity out of this whole peninsula. Everything had to be planned, nothing left to circumstances. The rim of the cape, the original view and my building had to be a unity.' The Mayan and Zapotec ruins of Mexico provided inspiration for the base upon which the shells would sit. Podiums at these ancient sites lifted the temples above the forest canopy providing worshippers with a clear and breathtaking view of the heavens and their surroundings. In Sydney, the podium would lift the sails above the water and give visitors to the secular temple an equally heavenly outlook. Utzon's entry was one of the last received.

Zapotec ruins, Monte Albán, Mexico

The winner is ...

On the afternoon of 29 January 1957, in front of a hushed audience at the place of judging, Premier Cahill opened the envelope containing the judges' decision to find the paper inside bore no name, just a number, 218, the only identifier known to the judges. A second piece of paper matched numbers and names revealing the winner to be Jørn Utzon, age 38, of Hellebæk, Denmark. A Philadelphia group was awarded second prize for their nautilus shell inspired spiral design with stages in the middle and auditoriums, cafes and galleries wrapped around. A British company won third prize with a conventional design consisting of two buildings along the length of the site separated by a courtyard. Hurriedly prepared cost estimates also favoured Utzon's design with the initial estimate being $7 million compared to $10.8 million and $15.6 million for the second and third place designs. In their report, the judges said of the winning entry: 'The drawings submitted are simple to the point of being diagrammatic. Nevertheless, as we have returned again and again to the study of these drawings, we are convinced that they present a concept of an Opera House which is capable of being one of the great buildings of the world.' The judges had chosen the imaginative over the predictable, a design that would stretch the limits of possibility.

Celebrations in Hellebæk

A phone call from a journalist in faraway Australia propelled ten-year-old Lin Utzon to jump on her bicycle and pedal after her father who was enjoying a morning walk in the beech forest near the family's Hellebæk home. The life-changing news delivered by the journalist to a breathless Jørn Utzon would be confirmed later by official cable. Friends and neighbours joined the Utzons that afternoon to celebrate the win which came just four weeks after the birth of Jørn and wife Lis's third child, Kim. Utzon had won his eighth competition, but this one was more than a prize: according to the rules, as winner, he was automatically the preferred choice to act as design architect charged with bringing the project to reality.

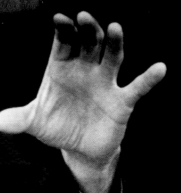

'It will give simple people pleasure.' Buckminster Fuller

'This circus tent is not architecture.' Frank Lloyd Wright

Letters to the Editor, *The Sydney Morning Herald,* 31 January 1957:

'At last! A clean refreshing breeze has found its way into the musty corridors of Australian architectural thought.'

'There is one consolation. Although it looks like a disintegrating circus tent in a gale, the building is estimated to cost up to £4,000,000; and that consideration alone will almost certainly ensure that it will not be erected for some considerable time to come, if at all.'

'To me, the winning design suggests some gargantuan monster which may have wandered over the land millions of years ago.'

'It is all very well to chatter about the thing causing an artistic furore, but it is well to remember that the people who have to pay for it will also have to live with it, and, if at some suitably remote period, our descendants regain any sense of taste or proportion, they will be forced to foot the bill for removing it and putting up something less repellent.'

27

The philosopher engineer

In Dublin, the day after the announcement in Sydney, Ove Arup, the British born son of a Danish father and Norwegian mother, was having breakfast when an article in *The Times* about the future Sydney Opera House, designed by a Dane, caught his eye. Eleven years earlier, Arup, educated in Germany and Denmark, first in philosophy and mathematics and later in engineering, had set up a structural engineering company in London. By 1957 Ove Arup & Partners had offices in England, Ireland and a number of African countries and was fast developing an enviable reputation. Arup sent a letter of congratulations to Utzon and offered the services of his company which could boast that one of the partners, Ronald Jenkins, was a leading authority on the calculation of shell structures. Arup added a postscript: 'If you don't know

who the hell I am you may think it very odd that I write to you. You may be right!'

Within days of the announcement of the competition results, Martin and Saarinen met Utzon in London and sent word back to Sydney that they believed he was 'admirably equipped to deal with all matters of design' although he would need help in financial management and the calculation of the complicated shell system. They also introduced Utzon to their and Ashworth's choice for the project's structural engineer, the man who had written to Utzon a few days before, Ove Arup. Twenty-four years Utzon's senior, Ove Arup had a reputation for working closely with architects to absorb the aesthetics of a project with the aim of blending the art and engineering into a total design. Impressed by the man and his philosophy, Utzon agreed that Ove Arup was the engineer for the complex job.

Architecture or sculpture?

Utzon's shell roof design was both celebrated and derided as sculpitecture, a blend of architecture and sculpture. Shell roof technology had advanced over previous decades with such structures becoming quite fashionable in the 1950s, Berlin's Congress Hall and Saarinen's TWA Terminal being the latest examples. A shell roof is a thin, rigid, curved surface in which forces act at a tangent to the surface of the shell. As such, any shell roof design must be mathematically precise so the force of gravity acts through the shell material down to the supports.

Utzon's huge shells were not described geometrically, they were freeform. No one was sure they could be built the way he envisaged them. Investigations would involve extraordinarily large numbers of calculations in an era when there were few computers in the world and engineers worked with slide rules, logarithm tables and hand-cranked adding machines. Nothing about the shells would be easy.

A big gamble

With the architect on board, the task now for Premier Cahill was to rally support amongst his own Labor Party and the general public to get the project funded and underway. An election two years away placed considerable urgency on the task as Cahill believed a change of government would see the whole thing shelved. To prevent such an undesirable outcome, the Premier informed Utzon that the Opera House project, if it was to start at all, must start by February 1959. A deadline had been set.

Now it was just a matter of getting the money. When it came to promoting the concept to the average taxpayer who was far more likely to patronise a cricket match or horse race than an opera performance, Cahill wished the project had been assigned a less elitist sounding name; after all, opera would be only one of a number of offerings staged in the theatres. Sydney Concert Hall or Sydney Entertainment Centre would have been much easier to sell. But Opera House it had been from the beginning and Opera House it would remain. How then to raise funds without alienating the voters? Donations from the well-heeled members of Sydney society, the very people who would attend the symphony and opera, would pay a small part of the cost. Some tax revenue could be allocated to the project, but not too much. The key to raising the balance was the demonstrated willingness of the citizens of New South Wales to take a punt. In May 1957 Cahill announced that the Opera House would be funded by a special lottery, drawn four times a year until the project was paid off. The estimated $900,000 in lottery revenue before work began would be supplemented with only $200,000 of taxpayer funds. The Opera House Lottery with a first prize of $200,000 was launched later in the year with tickets costing $10. The first draw was held on 10 January 1958 with the $200,000 prize going to one of Sydney's wealthiest citizens.

Utzon comes to town

On the night of 29 July 1957, Jørn Utzon arrived in Sydney to visit the site and meet Premier Cahill and members of the Sydney Opera House Executive Committee. 'It's absolutely breathtaking,' Utzon said the next day on a blustery Bennelong Point, 'There is no opera site in the world to compare with it.' He went on to say of his roof design: 'In Berlin recently, I saw a congress hall with such a roof spanning about two hundred and forty feet, and it was only three inches thick.' The three-week-long visit was well covered in the media and the people of Sydney were quickly charmed by the tall Dane with film-star looks.

After meeting with Utzon, Cahill announced that the foundation stone for the Opera House would be placed in early 1959 and that Ove Arup and Partners had been appointed consulting engineer. Fundraising began on 7 August at Sydney Town Hall with Cahill handing over the government's contribution of $200,000 and then donating $100 himself. An additional $270,000 was raised that evening including $600 from the sale of kisses in the Lord Mayor's reception room. Utzon donated $100 to kiss the cheek of flautist Elaine Schaffer and another $100 to kiss the wife of celebrated violinist Ruggiero Ricci. Mrs Ricci offered $20 to kiss the ABC's Charles Moses who was so thrilled he kicked in $100 himself.

The Red Book

Upon returning to Denmark, Utzon engaged a number of consultants to help him prepare a more detailed outline of the project. Mogens Balslev was appointed consultant on electrical installation; Vilhem Jordan on acoustics; Sandro Malmquist on theatre techniques; and Jorgen Varming on mechanical and air-conditioning systems. Meanwhile Ove Arup's company went about working on methods of constructing the roofs.

Reports from the various consultants were assembled in the Red Book which Utzon, accompanied by Arup, delivered to Premier Cahill and the Opera House Executive Committee in March 1958. An inscription by Utzon inside the book expressed the view that '... the scheme can be crystallised in a building which, in a functional, festive and inspiring manner will shelter the activities and life lived within it, and in so doing enhance the face of Sydney.'

Arup defined the shells as a series of symmetrical coaxial parabolas joined at a ridge along the top. The shells curved the way a stone thrown horizontally off a cliff will curve as it falls to earth: flat at the top, steep at the bottom. Arup advised that preliminary calculations indicated considerable bending moments in high wind and recommended extensive model testing to check the theory.

Jordan's report in the Red Book outlined the acoustic problems associated with a dual purpose hall and how they may be overcome. The major hall would need to accommodate the differing reverberation times required by symphony concerts and grand opera. Reverberation time is the time from the emission of a sound until its absorption by the air, auditorium surfaces and audience. Jordan estimated reverberation times based on a major hall volume of $11m^3$/seat to be 1.8-2.0s for symphony concerts and, with part of the hall screened off, 1.6-1.8s for grand opera.

He described a hall as a coupled enclosure: stage area and seating area. If too much sound energy is trapped on stage, there is a deficiency in the seating area; if too much sound energy is distributed towards the audience, there is a lack on the stage itself which causes difficulties for the conductor and musicians who must hear the music they are playing. He hoped to find the correct balance for the Sydney auditoriums. He described the acoustic properties of a number of halls including Royal Festival Hall in London with a volume $6.6m^3$/seat and a reverberation time of 1.8s empty and 1.5s with an audience,

EAST ELEVATION   SCALE 1/32"

and Aalborghallen in Denmark with 14m³/seat and a reverberation time of 3.0s empty and 1.9s with an audience. As for electronic amplification, none would be necessary for symphony concerts in the major hall, but single performers would require a delay amplification system whereby the sound emanating from speakers along the length of the hall would be electronically delayed by the necessary fraction of a second to match the live sound travelling from the front at 340m/s.

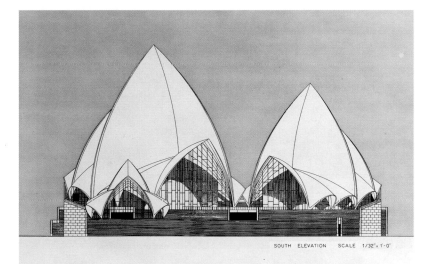

SOUTH ELEVATION   SCALE 1/32"=1'-0"

He recommended the installation of acoustic panels on the upper side and back walls which could be changed or adjusted to fine tune reverberation time. As for the minor hall which would host drama and intimate opera, applications requiring clear articulation, Jordan suggested reverberation times between 1.3 and 1.6s. He described how a model could be used to test acoustics. Recorded music played on stage inside a 1:10 scale model at ten times its normal speed and recorded in the seating area would, when played back at normal speed, give a good indication of the real hall acoustics. Acoustic details for the drama theatre, chamber music studio, rehearsal rooms, foyers and restaurant were also outlined as was sound dampening for services such as lifts, fans and water pipes. On the large scale, Jordan outlined design features such as separate foundations for the two halls and two structural layers per hall to minimise sound transmission between halls and keep out ship and aircraft sounds.

In his report on theatre technique, Malmquist outlined how the small wing space of the Opera House stages provided opportunities far more interesting than the normal practice of wheeling scenery on stage behind a closed curtain. 'We have broken out of the snail-shell of the baroque theatre and have discovered so many more ways in which to play theatre.' Planes raised and lowered by hydraulic lifts would produce a rich and dynamic space on the Opera House stage. And the lift system would meet the demands of modern producers who wanted scene shifting to take place during the performance itself. He described how Shakespeare's *Hamlet*, a play requiring between 20 and 25 shifts of scenery, could be performed simply with sculptural or abstract scenery representing nothing particularly recognisable, but brought to life by the actors. Abstract banquet hall scenery could be lowered at the same time as the ramparts of Kronborg Castle were raised behind the actors. This would provide a novel and dramatic effect. And with stage basement space considerably larger than normal wing space, there would be room for even more sets. In addition, the platform lifts allowed for versatility. Platforms could be lifted above or below the normal stage level allowing various configurations. For example, the stage level could be set at the level of the theatre floor eliminating the boundary between stage and auditorium. A variation of this would have some audience seating on raised platforms at the back of the stage, behind the performers. The possibilities were exciting.

Varming produced diagrams of the ventilation system for the complex which would provide fresh air at a rate of $57m^3$/person/hour. He likened the shells to parasols which would insulate the halls from solar radiation thereby making air-conditioning a simpler task than it would be in a conventional theatre. Fans, vents, air-conditioning and boiler units would be designed and positioned to minimise noise within the theatres.

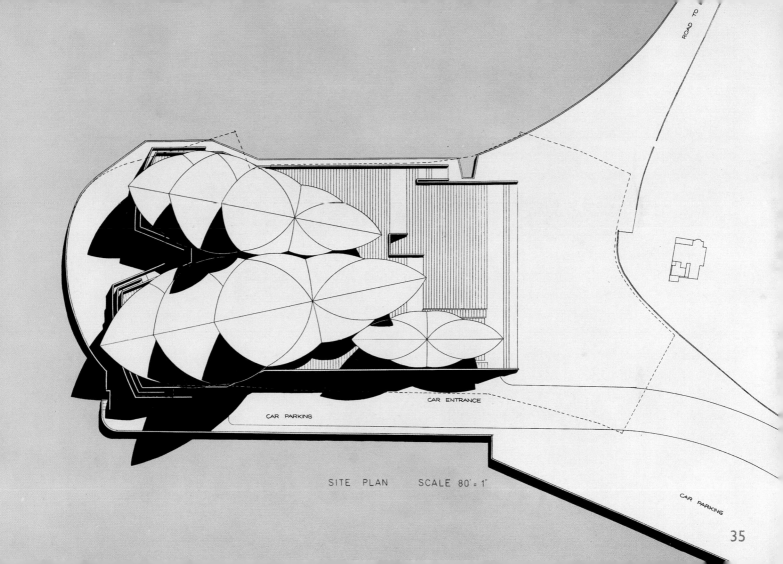

SITE PLAN   SCALE 80'= 1"

Orchestras and operas

During his March 1958 visit, Utzon met with the ABC's Charles Moses and Hugh Hunt, Executive Director of the Elizabethan Theatre Trust (now Opera Australia). As sponsor of the Sydney Symphony Orchestra, the ABC would be the primary client for the major hall, and as such, had a keen interest in the number of seats: more seats would mean more revenue per performance and fewer performances per year to satisfy the 10,000 subscribers. The Red Book provided for 2700 seats in the major hall with no balcony and 3000 seats with a balcony. Utzon recommended against the inclusion of a balcony for acoustic reasons, advice accepted by Moses on the condition that Utzon somehow fit additional seats to bring the capacity to 2850; this would be 500 more than Sydney Town Hall but still below the 3000 to 3500 originally proposed by Goossens. An audience of 1826 would be accommodated in grand opera mode by removing rows of seats at the front of the hall and hydraulically raising sections of floor to create the larger stage required. A later meeting saw the major hall numbers change to 2800 for concerts and 1700 for grand opera with row spacing of ninety centimetres. The minor hall would have a capacity of 1200 for drama and 1100 for opera which required additional space for an orchestra pit.

A beginning, an end

While Utzon and Arup returned to work in Europe, Cahill and the Sydney Opera House Executive Committee moved things forward in Sydney. Test bores were sunk at Bennelong Point to gauge the depth to bedrock and wind velocity and shipping noise at the site were monitored. On 18 August 1958 demolition work started on Fort Macquarie Depot. Utzon returned to Sydney in November with plans for what would be a three stage project. Tenders were called for Stage 1, the construction of the podium, and with the lowest bid of $2.8 million, Civil & Civic Contractors Pty Ltd was awarded the work.

The ceremony to mark the start of the project, 2 March 1959

Premier Cahill installs the inaugural plaque designed by Yuzo Mikami

THIS PLAQUE COMMEMORATES THE COMMENCEMENT OF
CONSTRUCTION OF THE   SYDNEY OPERA HOUSE
ALL MEASUREMENTS ARE TAKEN FROM THIS
BASIC REFERENCE POINT
THE PLAQUE WAS FIXED BY THE HONOURABLE
JOHN JOSEPH CAHILL M.L.A.
PREMIER OF NEW SOUTH WALES
ON THE SECOND DAY OF
MARCH 1959

On a rainy 2 March 1959, with Utzon present, Premier Cahill screwed a bronze plaque into place at what would be the first step of the podium and declared the project underway. The Leader of the Opposition in state parliament and Cahill's opponent in the upcoming election, Robin (later Robert) Askin, pledged his support to bring the 'magnificent concept into being'. Victorious at the election, Cahill announced that the Opera House would open on Australia Day, 26 January 1963. But Cahill would never see his Opera House. Seven months after placing the plaque, the sixty-eight year old dynamo fell ill from a bleeding gastric ulcer during a meeting at Parliament House. Refusing an ambulance, he was driven in his car to nearby Sydney Hospital where he was given a blood transfusion, but died after suffering a heart attack.

Stage 1: the podium

The rushed start to the project put a great deal of pressure on the Arup staff in London

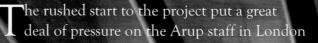

responsible for producing the working drawings required by Civil & Civic. Delays in London translated to down-time and frustration on site. Added to this were unforeseen problems. Bennelong Point was found to be less stable than it appeared. A good portion of the peninsula was rubble put down when Fort Macquarie was built and water intruded into the lower levels of what would become the foundations. In all, approximately 700 piers were needed to support the podium, far more than Civil & Civic had estimated. In addition, divers were needed to pump water from pier formwork, cofferdams had to be built to prevent water seeping into concrete work deep inside the podium, and the foundations of an old ferry terminal had to be blasted out.

Stage 1 was completed in February 1963, two years behind schedule at a significant loss to Civil & Civic. The finished podium consists of a reinforced concrete monolith out of which the seating for the two theatres appears to be scooped. The most notable technical feature is the design of the single-span concrete beams, some 49m long, which are visible below the concourse stairway and many other places within the podium. The change in cross-sectional shape from U at each end of a beam to T in the middle provides the necessary strength while the upper surface trough provides water drainage from the flat podium surface. Civil & Civic were later successful in a claim for unforseen work amounting to $2.5 million, almost doubling the tendered amount.

As Stage 1 proceeded, Cahill's successor, Robert Heffron announced the formation of the Sydney Opera House Trust which would be responsible for the long term operation of the working complex; an Austrian company, Waagner Biro, was awarded the contract for construction and installation of the stage machinery at a price of $3.4 million; cost estimates for the project went from $9.6 million, to $13 million, to $25 million, and the completion date from January 1963 to late 1965.

Resin coated plywood forms for concourse beams

40

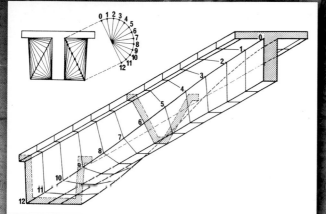

Cross-section of half-length of concourse beam. The U shape at the ends where the beam is supported places most concrete at the bottom where it is needed, while the T shape in the middle places most concrete at the top where it is needed. The transition from U to V to T and back is by way of a sine curve on each side of the beam, like a long wave in a calm sea

The spherical solution

While work on Stage 1 progressed, Arup and Utzon continued to plan Stage 2, the construction of the roof shells. Utzon had originally imagined the shells being cast in situ. Scaffolding of a gigantic extent would be erected to hold formwork of the required shape. Reinforcing steel would be placed on top of the formwork and concrete poured and shaped. When the scaffolding was removed, the shell would support itself, much like a dome or arch. Computer assisted stress calculations were

carried out with the shells described geometrically, first in parabolic terms and later as ellipsoids. While a parabola is the path taken by an object thrown into the air, an ellipse is the path of an object in orbit, for example a satellite around the earth or the earth around the sun. An ellipsoid is an ellipse in three dimensions. Perspex models were made of the shells and tests undertaken with various weight loadings and inside a wind tunnel. When these tests revealed shear forces and bending moments higher than expected, the scheme was changed to two shells 1.2m apart, separated by a web. This too was

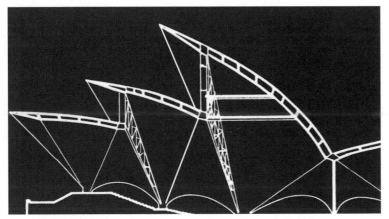

Parabolic scheme

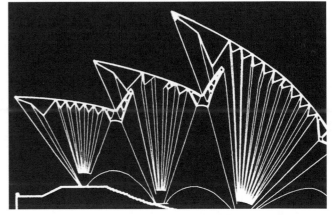

Ellipsoid scheme

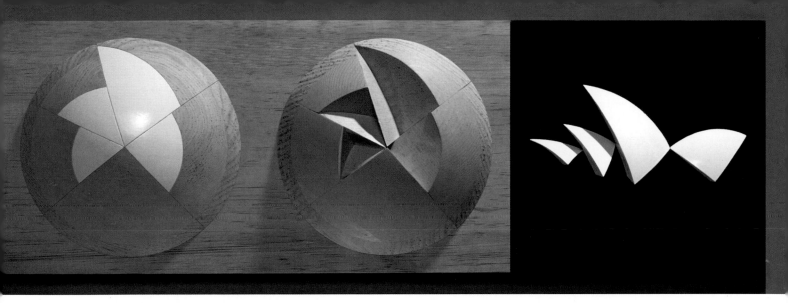

dismissed on the basis of test results, the fear being that if one of the interconnected shells collapsed in a freak gale, failure of adjacent shells would follow. Steel framework with concrete skins offered a stronger alternative but was dismissed by Utzon as dishonest since the concrete served no structural purpose. A completely different approach with roofs made from giant prefabricated concrete ribs offered a solution but at a prohibitive cost due to the very large number of forms required to accommodate the change in curvature over the ellipsoid surfaces. And then, a stroke of genius! Prefabricated ribs, each part of a sphere rather than an ellipsoid, could be made with just a few forms. To demonstrate the spherical solution, Utzon had a local shipyard carve his concept in wood. The roofs could be built, but their profile was now significantly different to that in the original competition entry and the Red Book. Would the client approve of the new look with changed clearances and hall volumes?

The Yellow Book

In March 1962, Utzon, accompanied by Arup engineer Jack Zunz, flew to Sydney via the United States carrying drawings and details of the spherical solution in what became known as the Yellow Book. Delays in assembling the drawings had forced a change to their original itinerary, a minor setback which saved their lives. Tragically, on 1 March, the American Airlines 707 they had been booked on from New York to Los Angeles crashed on take-off killing all 97 people aboard.

The design modifications outlined in the Yellow Book were accepted by Minister for Public Works, Norman Ryan. There would be three shell systems, one over the major hall, one over the minor hall and one over the restaurant. The shells would be made of ribs each of which was a narrow triangular shape cut from a sphere of radius 75m. The ribs would be cast on site in forms, properly called beds, which would be reused. The shells would be independent. Should one fail, the others would not. The contract for the construction of the shells was awarded to M.R. Hornibrook (NSW) Pty Ltd in October 1962. The terms of the contract with Hornibrook were quite different to those with Civil & Civic. Hornibrook would be paid a flat $150,000 management fee with the government paying all labour, plant and material costs.

47

A royal welcome

On 4 March 1963, Utzon, accompanied by his wife and children, arrived in Sydney as migrants after enjoying a relaxing ten week holiday in the United States and Tahiti. Coincidentally, the royal yacht *Britannia* with Queen Elizabeth and Prince Phillip on board was in Sydney Harbour, not far from the Opera House site which the Queen and Prince had toured two days earlier. Upon being made aware of the architect's imminent arrival, Her Majesty expressed the desire to meet him before *Britannia* sailed for Brisbane that night. A radio call to the French aircraft and a waiting car at the airport saw Utzon and wife, still in their travelling clothes, lunching with the royal couple an hour after touching down.

Arup and Hornibrook were also pleased to see Utzon in Sydney. The difficulty in contacting the architect during his travels had forced them to make decisions about Stage 2 without his consent, something they would rather not have done. From now on, communication would not be a problem. Utzon was in Sydney, in an office at Bennelong Point, right next to the Arup office headed by Michael Lewis.

Problems at Bennelong Point

The first issue to be addressed in Stage 2 was a direct result of the hurried start to the project. The podium, correctly built by Civil & Civic, had been designed to support thin concrete shells, not the heavy pre-cast ribs of the spherical solution. In order to accommodate the extra weight, twenty or so piers would have to be blasted apart to expose reinforcing steel and concrete poured to a greater diameter. So as not to attract unwanted attention, the explosions were carried out during peak traffic times, a ruse that was eventually exposed by the media.

This story, in addition to those on cost escalation and delays at Bennelong Point, placed a great deal of pressure on everyone involved in the project. Arup, for one, thought it unreasonable that his company was being criticized for problems that were the direct result of the political decision to start the project before plans were complete, an unthinkable approach under less ambitious circumstances. And there were other reasons for concern. Because of Utzon's lack of experience with large projects, Arup had agreed to manage the contract. As a result, it was his company, not Utzon, who was responsible for paying consultants appointed by Utzon and answerable to him. Arup staff would pay an invoice submitted by a consultant and claim the money from the Department of Public Works with no guarantee that all that was claimed would be paid. In addition, the Sydney Opera House project was placing considerable pressure on Arup's resources at the expense of other work. By the end of 1962, fifty-five engineers and support staff had spent 175,000 hours on the project with a considerable amount of the time spent on the preparation of working drawings which were normally the task of the architect. The scrapping of thousands of hours of intense work with each roof design revision had caused considerable frustration in the London office and precipitated the resignation of shell expert Ronald Jenkins from the project. In March 1963 Ove Arup wrote to Minister Ryan outlining his concerns and requesting changes in the organisation of the project to take some of the load off his company. He reminded Ryan of a clause in the Brown Book stating that the winning architect may be required to enter into an agreement with another architect to design and supervise the work jointly with him. Arup praised Utzon and outlined the difficulties of the job, saying, 'He is no ordinary architect, and this is no ordinary job ...', that, 'Utzon must remain the leader...' , and, 'What we want is to do our utmost to make Utzon's dream come true, at whatever cost to ourselves, as long as we can bear it.' The Minister agreed to a new arrangement whereby Arup's company would work closely with Utzon who would take over the responsibility for payment of consultants and preparation of working drawings.

In September 1963, with Stage 1 finished and Stage 2 underway, the Sydney Opera House Executive Committee created a major problem for Utzon by rejecting a previously accepted plan to have 900 seats behind the orchestra in the major hall. The ABC had developed concerns about filling seats behind the orchestra. To accommodate the ABC, Utzon created three tiers of steeper seating which permitted the cantilevering of additional seating space over the outside stairs, and he reduced the distance between rows to allow more rows. The steeper seating raised the auditorium floor above the concrete podium upon which it was designed to sit and decreased air volume in the hall to the detriment of reverberation time. The decreased volume meant a redesigned ceiling, one without adjustable panels to vary air space to accommodate the different acoustic requirements of orchestra and opera. This was a major compromise to the dual purpose concept.

Stage 2: manufacturing the ribs

Each roof rib, from the shortest above the restaurant to the longest above the major hall, consists of segments made in one of three types of 23m-long, resin-coated, steel-reinforced plywood beds. Consider the process to make the longest ribs: to start, pre-made concrete diaphragms were placed vertically in the first bed dividing it into five segments of equal length numbered 1 to 5 with 1 being the segment that would eventually form the bottom of the rib. Reinforcing steel was placed and concrete poured into the segments and allowed to cure, the concrete diaphragms becoming the tops and bottoms of the rib segments. The segments were then removed from the bed and numbers 1 to 4 were stored ready for installation. Segment 5 was then placed in the second bed in position 1, the diaphragms were installed and the concrete poured. After curing, segment 5 from this pour became segment 1 in the third bed. This sequence produced thirteen segments (5+4+4), the maximum required, with the concrete diaphragms ensuring a perfect fit from one segment to the next. To speed production, Hornibrook used multiple beds, and when storage space became a problem, rib segments were sent to a very safe holding yard: the garden at Long Bay prison.

Stage 2: constructing the shells

The warped side shell arches were built first and the pedestals upon which the ribs would radiate were constructed off them, the concrete poured in situ. Rib segments were lifted into position by one of three 75m high, French-made, rail-mounted tower cranes. Once in place, segments were supported by an ingenious steel erection arch developed by Hornibrook which did away with the need for massive scaffolding structures. Each of the four telescopic erection arches used on site could be shaped to match the curve of the shell as it moved out. For example, rib 2 was constructed supported on one side by completed rib 1, and on the other by the erection arch in the shape of what would be rib 3. Wide pins across the back of each rib segment prevented it falling through the gap. When rib 2 was finished, the erection arch would be pivoted and shaped to match what would be rib 4, allowing the construction of rib 3. The rib segments were glued together with epoxy resin, a novel technique endorsed by Arup and Hornibrook after stress tests saw concrete fracture before the resin joint. Rib segments were stressed during construction with nine steel cables running from the first segment to the top segment. When all segments of a rib were in place, up to twenty-one additional cables were stressed in three locations from the pedestal to the crown with additional cables running horizontally between ribs. The last of the 2194 rib segments was lifted into position at the top of the major hall on 17 January 1967.

The warped side shell arches were constructed first

*The pedestals from which
the ribs would radiate
were constructed off the
warped side shell arches*

61

Stage 2: a million tiles

Utzon visualized the shells in striking contrast to the dark water under the deep blue Australian sky. They would be tiled, white, like clouds or sails on the water. And at night, the sails would 'glimmer in the dark'. The tiles must have gloss but not be so mirror-like to cause glare. He found exactly what he wanted in Japan, ceramic bowls with a subtle coarseness caused by a granular texture in the clay. Three years work by Höganäs of Sweden produced the effect Utzon wanted in what became known as the Sydney tile, 120mm square, made from clay with a small percentage of chamotte.

Utzon ruled out the individual placement of tiles by workers tethered to the shell in the belief that such a difficult and uncontrollable procedure would produce an uneven surface. He would apply the principle of additive architecture: prefabrication and repetition. The tiles would be assembled into lids of exactly the right curvature with equal spacing between tiles. The lids would then be lifted into position and attached to bolts and brackets already installed in the ribs.

The 4228 tile lids required to cover the shells were produced in a factory set up under the concourse stairway. Tiles were placed face down in one of twenty-six chevron shaped beds each with a base shaped to match the curve of the roof. Buff coloured tiles with a matt surface bordered glazed off-white ones to interact, in Utzon's words, like 'snow and ice'. Heated animal glue was poured into the gaps between tiles and allowed to solidify before three layers of galvanised steel mesh were placed and mortar poured and worked to the required thickness. The ingenious use of animal glue to prevent mortar seeping between tiles was proposed by a worker who was paid $100 for the idea. When a lid was steam cured overnight, the animal glue would melt leaving a clean groove between adjacent tiles which was sealed with epoxy. Finally, polyurethane foam insulation was spread over the back of the lid.

Lids were lifted into position by crane to be attached to the corresponding rib segment by means of pre-fitted corrosion resistant aluminium-bronze brackets and phosphor-bronze bolts. While installation was problem free for the lower lids, small manufacturing errors and deformations upon curing resulted in a rib and lid hardware mismatch higher up. The lids didn't fit. To overcome this problem, a team of surveyors undertook the tedious task of pinpointing the position of thousands of rib bolts on the already constructed shells. This data was entered into a computer which calculated the exact position of the bolts in space and provided the matching lid hardware configuration. Hardware was removed from the mismatched lids, recast and refitted. When a lid was lifted into position, the workers would be prepared with the correct number of packing pieces to produce a perfect curve from one lid to the next. The joints between lids were sealed with monolastomeric on a plastic backing strip which allowed for thermal movement.

'The sun did not know how beautiful its light was,
until it was reflected off this building.'   Louis Kahn

One roof, ten shells

Consider the roof of the major hall: shells 1 and 2, known as A1 and A2 in the design, stand back to back on their own legs. The side shells filling the space between them, 5 and 6, are in fact one structure supported by a cross-wall in the middle. This side shell structure was the first built with shells 1 and 2 erected from it. The whole shell 1 and 2 back-to-back unit stands on six legs and is independent of shell 3 to the north. Shell 3 stands on its own legs and is back to back with louvre shell 9, rising backwards into the mouth of shell 2. Shell 3 and the louvre shell are joined by side shell 7. This shell unit stands on four legs. Shell 4 is back to back with louvre shell 10 with side shell 8 between them. The minor hall is covered by a smaller version of the major hall roof and the restaurant roof is just one pair of back-to-back shells. Although the word 'shell' accurately described the early roof designs where comparison to the strong, thin shell of an egg could be made, it is not appropriate for the ribs; nevertheless, the word has stuck and the vaults, as they would be better known, are generally called shells.

4.   10.   3.   9.   2.   1.

8.   7.   6.   5.

As Stage 2 progressed, Arup's Michael Lewis and Minister Ryan developed concerns about the slow pace at which Utzon was producing working drawings for Stage 3: the interiors, glass walls and podium cladding. Lewis believed that Utzon did not have enough staff to produce the drawings at the rate they would be needed, that he was not set up to deal with the complexities of the job. To better gauge progress at the site, on 5 March 1964, Ryan appointed Bill Wood, a supervising architect from his department, as liaison architect for the project, an appointment not entirely welcomed by Utzon who saw it as interference. That month also saw the start of a long industrial dispute over the sacking of four crane drivers. In June 1964, when Ryan announced a new price tag of $34.8 million and a completion date of March 1967, the Opposition demanded a royal commission be appointed to investigate the cost escalations and delays at Bennelong Point.

In August, the hall ceilings became a major issue. For years Utzon had been working with Ralph Symonds Ltd of Sydney, a world leader in the manufacture of large sheet plywood. Utzon's ceilings would consist of giant boxes each made from a single sheet of plywood, lead lined for sound insulation and hot bonded to aluminium reinforcement, the undersides convex, as if sliced from a cylinder. The airtight boxes would be carried to the site by barge and hoisted into position. Symonds had worked with Utzon to the extent of manufacturing prototype units on the basis that they would get the work. When Utzon requested funding for Symonds to make a mock-up of the minor hall ceiling, Ryan refused, suggesting that such funding would jeopardise the principle of competitive tendering. The requirement for subcontract tenders was not new, the supply of tiles had been subject to tender. Complications were avoided in that instance when Höganäs, the company Utzon had worked with, came in cheapest. The Sydney Opera House Executive Committee sided with Utzon on the plywood ceiling issue, suggesting that it was not unusual for an architect to nominate a subcontractor and that after all, Symonds was the only company capable of making the large sheets required, up to 15m long. This seemed to make little difference to the Department of Public Works who suggested that Symonds make their research available to competitors to assist them in the tendering process. Another level of uncertainty was introduced when Symonds was placed in receivership. Utzon needed Symonds to fulfill his concept of unity of materials. He planned on using plywood to line many of the rooms and hallways of the complex and Symonds had developed a metal-encapsulated tubular plywood product to support the huge glass curtains under the shells. Utzon had also been working with Concrete Industries, a subsidiary of Monier, to produce evenly coloured reconstituted granite facing for the podium to give it the appearance of one massive rock.

Concrete Industries were also working under the assumption that they would get the work.

Later in the year Waagner Biro of Vienna delivered hundreds of tonnes of stage machinery as specified, on time, but before the shells were ready to receive it. The additional expense of leasing large air-conditioned storage to protect the machinery from corrosion provided the media with another story of waste at Bennelong Point.

In November 1964, in the hope of recreating the peace and quiet of Hellebæk, Utzon set up a second office in a rented boat shed at Palm Beach to the north of Sydney. There, without even a telephone, he worked with a small select team three days a week. Life at Bennelong Point was not so calm. Strains had developed in the relationship between Utzon and Arup staff to the extent that Ove Arup travelled to Sydney and offered to withdraw from the project to allow Utzon a fresh start with a new engineer. The offer was not accepted by Utzon who had no wish to work with anyone but Arup.

A change of government

The goings on at Bennelong Point were a major issue leading into the 1965 election which Labor lost to a Liberal-Country Party coalition under the leadership of Robin Askin. Askin had promised to 'get some sense into the Opera House' by introducing a businesslike approach. Although lottery revenue had more than matched costs to date, there was no guarantee that situation would continue. Askin appointed the member for the rural seat of Armidale, Davis Hughes, as Minister for Public Works. Hughes spent days and nights going over the Opera House files. He learned that the latest estimate of $34.8 million was low and that there was little in the way of working plans for Stage 3. He put his staff to work on a new cost estimate and appointed an on-site watchdog, the recently retired Public Works director, R. A. Johnson, a move seen by Utzon as a challenge to his integrity. The revised estimate of $49.4 million announced in August prompted Hughes to rule that all future expenditures must be approved by him, and that absolutely all future work would be put out to tender. Utzon could not see how such an inflexible approach could work in a project as revolutionary as the Opera House.

Utzon leaves the job

Under Minister Ryan, Utzon had been given monthly advances to pay his staff and meet running costs. Hughes altered the arrangement, insisting that Utzon provide evidence of plans for Stage 3 before payments would be made. Utzon did have plans for Stage 3 but they were not all on paper. His preferred method of operation was to work with a talented contractor on a solution, one which would utilize repetitive elements, then have the contractor prepare the working drawings. This was at odds with Hughes's requirement.

In January 1966 a report by Arup's Michael Lewis concluded that Utzon's auditorium ceilings were too heavy and proposed self-supporting steel structures covered with plywood, an idea which Utzon had looked at earlier and rejected for acoustic reasons. Utzon dismissed Lewis's report and wrote to Ove Arup asking for his personal intervention, describing the situation in Sydney as 'very bad' and accusing Michael Lewis and staff of being unprofessional because they had gone behind his back and dealt directly with the client. Arup had always supported

Utzon, describing him as a 'brilliant designer ... probably the best of any I have come across in my long experience of working with architects.' Certainly when Arup was personally heavily involved in the project, he had dealt with Utzon only, never directly with the client. Arup replied to Utzon's letter saying that he had great faith in Michael Lewis and his staff at Bennelong Point, and that they and Utzon should work together, that united they could finish the job. Concerned that Utzon was toying with the idea of leaving the project, Arup counselled: 'If you resign, all is lost ...', that resignation or even the threat of resignation, 'would be a most dangerous thing even to think of it.'

On 24 February 1966 the ABC's acoustic engineer shocked Utzon with the announcement that, even with the latest changes, Sydney Opera House would not be a suitable venue for the Sydney Symphony Orchestra. A further blow to Utzon was a ruling by the Australian taxation office that he was not exempt from paying tax on earlier income which had already been taxed in Denmark. The double tax approximated his Sydney income.

On the morning of 28 February 1966, Utzon, believing he would be unable to pay his staff very much longer, went to Hughes's office and demanded the settlement of a claim he had submitted previously for $102,000 for consultancy work on stage machinery. Hughes responded that the claim was being investigated and that he would have an answer by the end of the week. It was the straw that broke the camel's back. Utzon left the meeting and immediately wrote to Hughes citing delays in payment of the $102,000 and a lack of collaboration as factors which forced him 'to leave the job', adding that he felt Hughes did not respect him as an architect. Without delay Hughes informed the press of Utzon's resignation saying it was 'a matter of regret', and that it was the government's intention to complete the building in the spirit of the original concept. The response was fast and intense, the Opera House itself seeming to react on 2 March when one of the telescopic arches collapsed barely missing six workers. On 3 March, 1000 people marched on Parliament House demanding Utzon's reinstatement. Patrick White, who would do about it,' adding, 'I have designed every line, every corner, every piece of surface. To kill the Opera House may take a long time. But it is dying and sick on the bed now.' Three days later the president people of Sydney he should 'turn the other cheek'. Zunz received no answer. Utzon wrote to Hughes on 15 March ruling out the Lane Cove proposal but offering to carry on as leader with the assistance a panel of architect consultants appointed by the Minister. He added, 'It is not I but the Sydney Opera House that created all the enormous difficulties.' The government was not about to compromise. The door finally closed on Utzon on 19 April when Hughes announced the appointment of a panel to finish the Opera House:

Utzon's model of the dual purpose major hall. The model also illustrates Utzon's ceiling and glass walls

Chief Government Architect E.H. Farmer would be chairman; thirty-four year old Peter Hall, a talented government architect, would be responsible for design; Lionel Todd from the private sector would be responsible for contracts; and David Littlemore, also from the private sector, would be supervising architect. Interestingly, Peter Hall had visited Utzon's office in Denmark during the early days of the Opera House project and applied for a job but was not hired because of the short length of time he was able to stay. Utzon terminated his staff, closed his office, and sent Hughes a bill for $480,000 for outstanding fees which Hughes promised to investigate. Utzon responded that he would not hand over plans for Stage 3 until the bill was paid. A compromise was later reached in which Utzon received $150,000 and handed over the drawings. On 24 April Ove Arup and Jack Zunz arrived in Sydney but Utzon did not see them. On 28 April, exactly two months after leaving the project, Utzon and family evaded reporters outside their home, travelled to the airport and boarded a Qantas flight for Honolulu minutes before it departed. Jørn Utzon would never return.

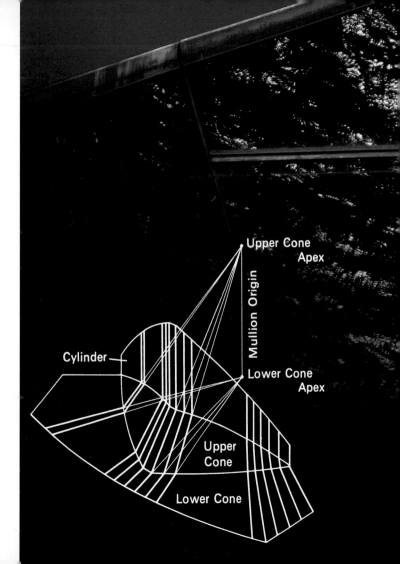

Stage 3: finishing the job

Upon returning from a twelve week study tour of concert halls and opera theatres overseas, Peter Hall proposed a major revision to the whole Opera House concept. He reported that the dual purpose concept was unworkable, that the major hall should be a concert hall and that opera should be relegated to the minor hall. This was shocking news for the Elizabethan Theatre Trust who argued that the major hall must host opera, a competition requirement that Utzon had not tried to evade. Pleased with Hall's revision, the ABC agreed that the Sydney Symphony Orchestra would be the primary client of the major hall as long as certain specifications were met.

In January 1967, after enlisting the help of American theatre consultant Ben Schlanger and Utzon's acoustic consultant Vilhem Jordan, the panel of architects presented the client with their *Review of Program*. The major hall would be a concert hall only with seating for 2800 and a reverberation time of 2.0s. The proscenium arch and stage tower already erected in the hall would be removed, and the large space under the stage designed for machinery would become a rehearsal room. Galleries would be added

to the minor hall increasing its capacity from 1100 to 1500, and the orchestra pit would be enlarged to accommodate eighty musicians. Reverberation time would be 1.3s, very suitable for opera. In an amazing about-turn by Hughes, the contract for Stage 3 was awarded, without tenders being called, to Hornibrook, a company very familiar with the difficulty of the project, with no completion date specified.

Hall, Todd and Littlemore's recommendations were accepted by Hughes and dismantling of the stage tower and proscenium arch began in June. Most of the major hall stage machinery was scrapped. Two years after their appointment, the panel of architects presented the first plans to Hughes who announced a new cost of $85 million and a completion date of 1972. Work went ahead at a rapid pace. Glass curtain walls in the shape of elliptical cylinder and cone sections were hung using structural steel framework inside and manganese-bronze corrosion-proof framework outside. The French-made sheets, consisting of a thin layer of demi-topaz glass heat bonded to plastic and thicker glass, were cut on site

Concert Hall

Sydney Symphony Orchestra with Maestro Vladimir Ashkenazy

to fit the complex geometry. The walls and ceiling of the Concert Hall were fabricated using Australian white birch plywood and floors and stairs throughout the complex were built with Australian brush box hardwood. John Olsen painted his *Five bells* mural which was later installed in the Concert Hall foyer overlooking the harbour, the scene of the drowning on which the mural is based.

On 17 December 1972 a symphony concert was held to test acoustics in the completed Concert Hall. Members of the Opera House Trust, invitees of the Minister for Public Works, architects, engineers and almost 2000 Hornibrook workers and partners sat in silence as six blanks were fired from a pistol on stage to test reverberation time which came in at the predicted 2.0s. The science over, the Governor, Premier Sir Robert Askin and Davis Hughes took their seats to hear the Sydney Symphony Orchestra play. On a windy Saturday, 20 October 1973, almost seventeen years after Utzon's design was selected, fourteen and a half years after Premier Cahill placed the inaugural plaque, millions watched from around the world as Queen Elizabeth II opened

Sydney's Opera House comparing it to the Pyramids of Egypt, but adding, 'The Opera House will have something the pyramids never had ... it will have life.' Aboriginal actor Ben Blakeney then appeared high on the Concert Hall roof and declared, 'I am Bennelong ... and my spirit and the spirit of my people lives.' Water and aerial displays followed in the afternoon with fireworks and a symphony concert that night attended by the Queen. Jørn Utzon was invited to be present at the festivities but did not attend. His name was not mentioned in any of the official speeches.

Opera Theatre

DOOR
12
STALLS
NO
ENTRY

Concert Hall, interior stairs

Concert Hall, northern foyer

Time heals

In 1999, Jørn Utzon accepted an invitation from then premier of New South Wales, Bob Carr, to develop a Statement of Design Principles which would be used as a permanent reference for the long-term conservation and management of Sydney Opera House, and for any redevelopment of the interiors as and when such work becomes necessary. Utzon said: 'It is right that we should be looking forward to the future of the Sydney Opera House and not back to the past.' The first of these projects, the Utzon Room, western colonnade and western foyer were completed by Utzon working with his architect son, Jan, and Australian architect Richard Johnson. Structural engineering on these projects was by a company very familiar with the history and complexities of Sydney Opera House, Arup, now firmly established in a number of Australian cities. Looking back on the events of the mid-1960s, Jørn Utzon noted: 'Luckily Ove Arup stayed on the job; otherwise it would never have been completed.' Arup and Utzon met only once after the turbulent days in Sydney, at a ceremony in 1978 at which Utzon was awarded the Royal Institute of British Architects Gold Medal. The engineer congratulated his estranged friend, they spoke briefly, and parted. Ove Arup died ten years later at the age of ninety-two.

World Heritage and a birthday wish

On 28 June 2007 Sydney Opera House was added to the UNESCO World Heritage List alongside universally treasured structures such as the Pyramids, the Taj Mahal and the Great Wall of China. It is the youngest cultural site ever to be added to the list and the only one with the architect alive at the time of the award. The UNESCO report stated: 'Sydney Opera House stands by itself as one of the indisputable masterpieces of human creativity, not only in the twentieth century but in the history of humankind.' Upon receiving the news, Utzon commented: 'The Sydney Opera House is so close to my heart and is such a great part of my life. ... To me it is a great joy to know how much the building is loved.' On 9 April 2008, the day Jørn Utzon turned ninety, hundreds of Opera House staff gathered on the Concert Hall stage and, backed by the Sydney Symphony Orchestra, sang 'Happy birthday to you' to the ailing architect in Denmark. It was a true and final expression of love and appreciation from Australia. Jørn Utzon died in his sleep on 29 November 2008.

Utzon Room, opened in 2004, tapestry designed by Jørn Utzon, woven by the Victorian Tapestry Workshop under the supervision of Jørn's daughter, Lin

'We almost won. But we didn't.
Why? Because Jørn Utzon's
design was a masterpiece.'

Robert Geddes, a member of the
Philadelphia group which won
second prize in 1957

'The groundbreaking Danish architect had constructed something well ahead of its time, far ahead of available technology and he persevered through extraordinary malicious publicity and negative criticism to build a building that changed the image of an entire country. It is the first time in our lifetime that an epic piece of architecture gained such universal presence.'

Frank Gehry

Facts, figures, trivia and tragedy

Seating capacities: Concert Hall, 2679 (579 behind orchestra); Opera Theatre, 1547; Drama Theatre, 544; Playhouse, 398; Studio, 220-324; Utzon room, variable; Forecourt, variable

Venue capacity: 7000 when fully staffed with all theatres full

Events per year: 2400 including 1700 live performances

Visitors: 4.5 million, with 1.1 million attending performances and 240,000 taking guided tours

Number of rooms: over 800 including performance spaces above, 5 rehearsal studios, 60 dressing rooms, 5 restaurants, 6 theatre bars

Podium: 1.8ha area, 95m wide at southern end, in two levels 9m and 15m above mean sea level. The podium occupies approximately 80% of the entire site

Highest shell: 54.6m above podium, the height of an 18 storey building, 67.4m above mean sea level, 9m higher than Sydney Harbour Bridge deck

Distance between Concert Hall north and south shell tips: 121m

Radius of roof sphere segments: 75m

Weight of all three roofs: 21,000t

Longitudinal axes (centre line of roofs): Major hall: 348°41'24"; Minor hall: 11°18'36". The axes meet at a plaque on the concourse stairway. The plaque was originally placed by Premier Cahill

Tiles: 1,056,000 on 4228 lids, total area 1.6ha, the largest lid is 10m x 2.3m with a mass of 4t

Workforce: Approximately 10,000 people of 32 nationalities worked on the project over the fourteen years

Construction accidents: No fatalities on site; a crane driver was killed off site. A rigger who fell 35m from a major hall stage tower was lucky enough to have his fall broken by metal mesh. The most serious accident on site occurred on 2 March 1966 when a major hall erection arch collapsed onto a roof 15m below. Six riggers jumped clear and were unhurt

Final cost: $102,000,000. The building was paid off in July 1975, almost entirely from proceeds of the Opera House Lottery

Utzon's fees: 4% of cost of work for which a consultant was involved, 6% of cost of work in which only he was involved. Utzon's staff members were paid from these fees which amounted to a little over $1.25 million

Other Utzon projects: Bagsværd Church in Copenhagen and, with son Jan, Kuwait National Assembly which opened in 1982 and was badly damaged in the Gulf War of 1991

In 1985 Utzon, although not an Australian citizen, was made an honorary Companion of the Order of Australia. In 2003 Utzon was awarded the Pritzker Architecture Prize, considered by architects to be the highest award in their field

Other Arup projects: Coventry Cathedral; Centre Georges Pompidou, Paris; Hongkong Bank, Hong Kong; Øresund Bridge linking Denmark and Sweden; Millennium Bridge, Tate Modern and 30 St Mary Axe (The Gherkin), London; National Museum, Canberra

Early days saw Premier Cahill's ambitious project dubbed the Taj Cahill

The first performance at the Opera House occurred in November 1960 when black American political activist and human rights campaigner Paul Robeson entertained workers with several songs during their lunch break

Bazil and Freda Thorne's joy at winning the Opera House Lottery on 1 June 1960 turned to heartbreak when their son, Graeme, aged 8, was kidnapped on his way to school five weeks later. The kidnapper phoned the Thorne household and demanded a ransom of $50,000 but panicked when he suspected the police were involved and did not make contact again. Graeme's body, wrapped in a blanket, was found five weeks later. Clever forensic work enabled the police to identify a suspect, Stephen Lesley Bradley, who was subsequently arrested in Ceylon en route to England and extradited to Australia where he was found guilty of the kidnapping and murder

Utzon's design for the house he hoped to live in at Bayview overlooking Pittwater to the north of Sydney was rejected by the Warringah Shire Council because it had three separate buildings, (sleeping, living and working), joined by pathways. Council regulations permitted only one building per block. A modified plan was approved but never built. Utzon went on to build Can Lis on Mallorca overlooking the Mediterranean instead

The 10,000 pipe Concert Hall organ, the largest mechanical organ in the world, was built by Sydneysider Ronald Sharp and completed in 1979 at a cost of $1.2 million

An early proposal to build a carpark in the parkland adjacent to the Opera House was 'green banned' by the Builders Labourers Federation because excavation work would have resulted in the destruction of several very old Moreton Bay Fig trees. A carpark in the form of a double helical coil set underground behind the Tarpeian cliff face was opened in 1993

Sydney Opera House is the subject of an opera, The Eighth Wonder, which premiered at Sydney Opera House in October 1995

Acknowledgements: Thanks to Peter Fenoglio to whom credit for the artistic design and layout of the book must go; Serafina, Jennifer, Rachel, Wayne and others at Sydney Opera House for their enthusiastic support; Diana and Louise of Lend Lease for tracking down Ern McQuillan's rare and wonderful Stage 1 images; Eric Sierins for his patient help selecting images from the many brilliant Stage 2 and 3 photographs taken by Max Dupain; Arup staff for providing engineering detail; Yuzo Mikami, who worked on the project with Utzon and Arup, for allowing the use of his beautifully detailed drawings; State Records New South Wales and National Library of Australia for historic images and documents; Tania Lopez for the perfect image of Monte Albán to illustrate a point; and Karen Fenoglio, Ellie Housden, Carradine Lucas, Kate McDonald and Bernadette Moy for reading the text and providing thoughtful suggestions.

References and further reading: *The Arup Journal*, October 1973; *The Sydney Morning Herald*, 1956-1973; *The Masterpiece, Jørn Utzon: a secret life*, Philip Drew; *Jørn Utzon, The Sydney Opera House*, Francoise Fromonot; *Ove Arup, masterbuilder of the twentieth century*, Peter Jones; *Utzon's Sphere: Sydney Opera House, how it was designed and built*, Yuzo Mikami; *The saga of Sydney Opera House*, Peter Murray; *Sydney Opera House*, Michael Pomeroy Smith; *Building a masterpiece: the Sydney Opera House*, Anne Watson; *The Other Taj Mahal*, John Yeomans

Image credits: Australian Broadcasting Corporation: page 15, photographer Alfredo Valentini; **Peter Fenoglio:** back cover (bottom right) and pages 57 (top),68,69; **Grønlund's Forlag Denmark:** page 23, photographer Mikkel Grønlund; **Tania Lopez:** page 24; **Max Dupain and Associates:** pages 27,28,40,41,42,45,50,51,52,53,54,55,56,58,59,60,62,63,64,65, 66,67,77, photographer Max Dupain; pages 87,90-91, photographer Eric Sierins; **Ern McQuillan:** pages 37,38 (top),43; **Yuzo Mikami:** drawings on ends and pages 27,41,44,46,61; **Michael Moy:** front cover, back cover (top and bottom left) and pages 1,2,3,4,5,6,7,8,9,13,17,20,25,38 (bottom),39,57 (bottom),71,73,75,78,79,88,89,93,94,96; **National Library of Australia:** page 10, *Portrait of Bennilong, a native of New Holland, who after experiencing for two years the luxuries of England, returned to his own country and resumed all his savage habits*, 1798, artist unknown, nla.pic-an9353128; page 12, *North view of Sydney, New South Wales*, 1825, Joseph Lycett, nla.pic-an7690819; **State Records New South Wales:** page 19, CGS-12702 (The Brown Book); pages 31-35, CGS-12707 (The Red Book); back cover and page 47, CGS-12708 (The Yellow Book); **Sydney Opera House:** pages 83,84, photographer Greg Newington; page 81, photographer Ross Honeysett; and page 85; **Sydney Symphony Orchestra:** page 82, photographer Keith Saunders

First published in Australia by:
Alpha Orion Press
P.O. Box 207
Ashgrove QLD 4060
Australia
alphaorionpress.com.au
publisher@alphaorionpress.com.au

Graphic design: Peter Fenoglio

Printed by Bookbuilders

For Kate

National Library of Australia
Cataloguing-in-Publishing Data

Moy, Michael
Sydney Opera House : idea to icon.

ISBN 9780958106627 (hbk.).

1. Sydney Opera House - History. 2. Sydney Opera House
- Design and construction. 3. Sydney Opera House. I. Title.

725.822099441

Other titles by Michael Moy:

Sydney Harbour Bridge: idea to icon
Story Bridge: idea to icon

SYDNEYOPERAHOUSE

Every purchase supports Sydney Opera House
sydneyoperahouse.com

Drawings by Yuzo Mikami

COMPETITION SCHEME
FREEHAND
SINGLE SKIN R.C. SHELL
TAKEN FROM COMPETITION DRAWING
BY JØRN UTZON

1957

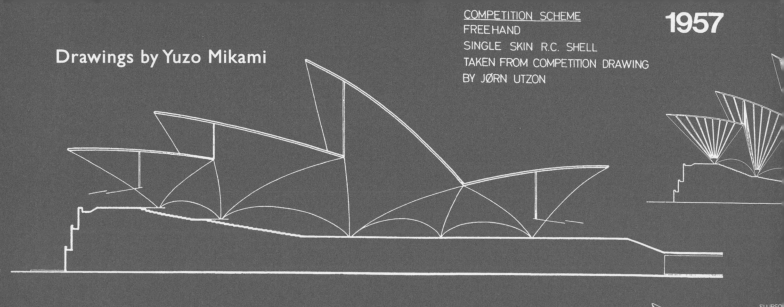

PARABOLIC SCHEME
PARABOLIC RIDGE PROFILE
PARABOLIC RIB PROFILE
DOUBLE SKIN R.C. SHELL WITH TWO-WAY
RIBS & STRUCTURAL LOUVRE WALL
SOH 402 DEC 1960

**1959
-61**

ELLIPSO
ELLIPTIC
ELLIPTIC
INSITU
1112 / S

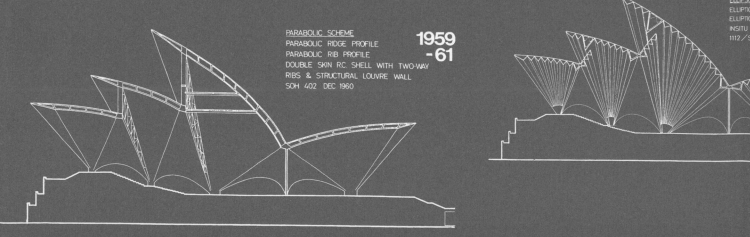